Stylish Shoes

for the Crafty
Fashionista

by Mary Meinking

FashionCraft
Studio

CAPSTONE PRESS
a capstone imprint

Snap Books are published by Capstone Press,
151 Good Counsel Drive, P.O. Box 669, Mankato, Minnesota 56002.
www.capstonepub.com

Books published by Capstone Press are manufactured with paper
containing at least 10 percent post-consumer waste.

Library of Congress Cataloging-in-Publication Data
Meinking, Mary.
 Stylish shoes for the crafty fashionista / by Mary Meinking.
    p. cm. — (Snap books. Fashion craft studio)
 Includes bibliographical references and index.
 Summary: "Step-by-step instructions for flip-flops, tennis shoes, and other shoe crafts made from
repurposed materials"—Provided by publisher.
 ISBN 978-1-4296-6554-4 (library binding)
 1. Shoes—Juvenile literature. 2. Clothing and dress—Remaking—Juvenile literature. I. Title. II. Series.

TT678.5.M45 2012
391.4'13—dc22   2011002451

 Editor: Mari Bolte
 Designer: Heidi Thompson
 Photo Stylist: Sarah Schuette
 Project Production: Marcy Morin
 Production Specialist: Laura Manthe

 Photo Credits:
 all photos by Capstone Studio/Karon Dubke

Printed in the United States of America in North Mankato, Minnesota.
032011   006110CGF11

Table of CONTENTS

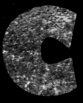
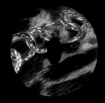

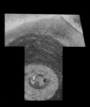

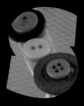

Thinking **Outside** the **Shoebox**

Shoes can elevate your wardrobe to the next level of fashion. Whether you're at the mall or hanging with the girls, why wear ordinary shoes? Kick things up a bit! What you put on your feet can be more than just the usual foot coverings.

Do you have some comfy but boring shoes hiding in the back of your closet? Don't toss 'em in the trash! Instead, give them a new look. Restyle your sneakers, dress shoes, flip-flops, boots, and even your slippers. Turn your worn-out wedges into fashionable footwear. Old flats can find new life with a bit of paint and glue. With a little creativity and some simple supplies around your house, you'll soon be stepping out in style.

The directions in this book are only ideas. You might not have the same shoes, fabric, trim, or decorations as shown. Don't worry about it! Let your inner designer create one-of-a-kind shoes your friends will envy!

Which Shoes to Restyle?

You probably won't want to restyle your favorite or most expensive shoes. Before redoing any of your shoes, it's best to check with your parents first.

If you don't have any old shoes to redo at home, hit the sale racks at your favorite stores. Resale boutiques, thrift stores, antique shops, and flea markets are treasure chests for secondhand clothes. Shoes ready to become today's trends could be waiting around the corner. And shopping for vintage kicks is a great way to spend a Saturday with your BFF!

Many art techniques won't work on dirty shoes, so make sure yours are clean. Wash canvas shoes in the washing machine. Don't use fabric softeners. Then let the shoes air dry completely. Foam flip-flops can be cleaned with a little soap and water. Use a cotton ball dipped in rubbing alcohol to clean leather, patent leather, or vinyl shoes.

It's easy to change measurements to metric! Just use this chart.

To change	into	multiply by
inches	centimeters	2.54
inches	millimeters	25.4
feet	meters	.305
yards	meters	.914

vintage—from the past

Flip-Flops that Pop

Make a splash at the beach, a pool party, or even the mall! These fun flip-flops are a great summertime project to make with friends. When you're done, use the leftover balloons to start a water fight with your friends!

You Will Need:

1 pair of flip-flops
110 small (5-inch) water balloons
permanent markers

1 Step one:
Lay balloons in a row to plan your color pattern.

Caution: Balloons can be choking hazards for small children. Keep them out of reach of anyone under age 3.

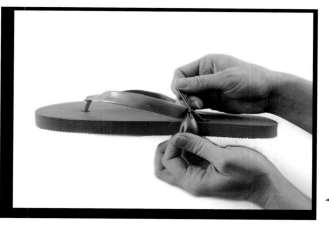

 **Step two:**
Tie balloons in a knot around flip-flop strap. Start on the sides of the flip-flop and work toward the center. Loose ends should face out.

 **Step three:**
Continue tying balloons, pushing them close together, until straps are covered. Repeat on other flip-flop.

 **Step four:**
Use markers to decorate the edge of the flip-flop's sole.

 Variation:
- Allergic to latex? Don't sweat it. Use bits of fabric, ribbons, or old T-shirts instead of balloons.

7

Wild Tie-Dye

Step back in time to the 1960s, when tie-dye was king. These shoes are easy to make, and you won't be scrubbing dye off your fingers for days. Rock this retro look during a night on the town.

You Will Need:

white canvas shoes
bucket, for soaking shoes
wide water-based markers
all-weather protective spray

Step one:

Test your shoes to make sure they will accept color. Put a couple drops of water on the shoes. If your shoes *absorb* the water, you can use them.

Tip: If your shoes don't absorb water, scrub them in hot water and soda ash. Soda ash is also called sodium carbonate or washing soda. The soda ash helps fiber hold dye. Soda ash can be found in the laundry aisle of your grocery store.

Step two:

Remove shoelaces and insoles (if they come out easily). Soak shoes in water until they're completely waterlogged.

Step three:

Using water-based markers, draw a pattern on wet fabric.

Step four:

Allow colors to bleed. Colors lighten when dried, so apply darker colors.

Tip: Avoid color combinations that look muddy when blended, such as blue-orange, red-green, or purple-red.

Step five:

Repeat on other shoe. If shoes dry before markers bleed together, lightly spray with water. Let shoes dry.

Step six:

Take shoes outside or to a well-ventilated room. Coat shoes with protective spray. Replace shoelaces and insoles.

❋ *Variation:*

- Tie-dye cotton shoelaces to match or contrast your shoes.

absorb—to soak up
insole—the inner lining of a shoe or boot

Cute as a Button

Update your old flip-flops with colorful treasures from the sewing basket. Fun buttons will transform your flip-flops into 3-D works of art. These flip-flops are as cute as a button!

You Will Need:

1 pair of flip-flops
about 30 flat buttons
vinyl or plastic adhesive
acrylic glitter paint

Step one:

Choose your flip-flops. They can be from the same pair, or you can mix and match to create your own style.

Step two:

Lay buttons in a row to plan your pattern.

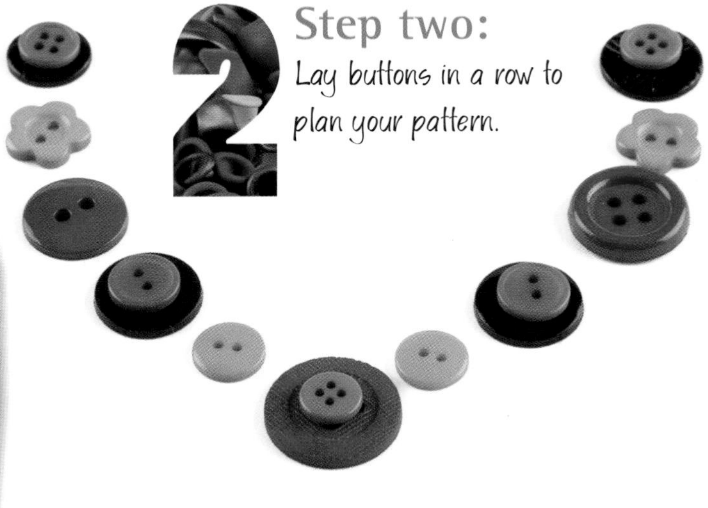

Step three:

Apply a few large dots of glue on the center of the strap. Place center button over glue and press until it holds.

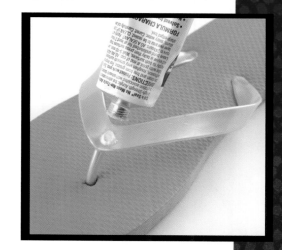

Step four:

Continue adding buttons down the straps. Overlap buttons, if desired.

✺ *Variation*:

• Buttons come in all shapes, sizes, and colors. Use different shapes to create a **theme** or letters to spell out words.

Step five:

Fill in strap areas between buttons with glitter paint. Let dry. Repeat with other flip-flop.

theme—a central idea that is reflected in decoration

Puddle **Jumpers**

Don't let rain keep you inside. Brave the weather and look great during a downpour. Grab some old rubber rain boots and give them new life. Your restyled boots will give a "splash" of color to your rainy days.

You Will Need:

pencil and paper
painter's tape
rubber rain boots
newspaper
fine sandpaper
paper towels
oil-based paint markers
vinyl or plastic adhesive (optional)
ribbon (optional)
buttons (optional)

 ## Step one:
Plan your design on paper.

Tip: Don't use acrylic paints or spray paints. The rubber will keep the boots from drying or will cause the paint to crack.

Step two:

Tape off areas on the boot you want to paint. Cover work surface with newspaper.

Step three:

Lightly sand exposed parts of the boot. Remove dust with a damp paper towel.

Step four:

Color untaped parts of the boots with markers. Let dry. Repeat with other boot.

Step five:

If you wish, glue ribbons or buttons on the boots.

Tip: Use oil-based markers outdoors or in a large area with the windows open.

A **Dab** Will Do Ya

Strokes of color will make your boring shoes dance for joy! Any design or color goes. You can decorate your shoes with modern or graphic art, hearts, flowers, stars, or even song lyrics. And if you change your mind, you can always paint over your old design. Shoes are a blank canvas, waiting for your artistic touch!

You Will Need:

paper, for sketching
pencil
light-colored canvas shoes
newspapers

acrylic paints
paintbrushes
permanent or fabric markers
all-weather protective spray

Step one:

Draw your design on paper. Use a pencil to redraw it on the canvas part of your shoes.

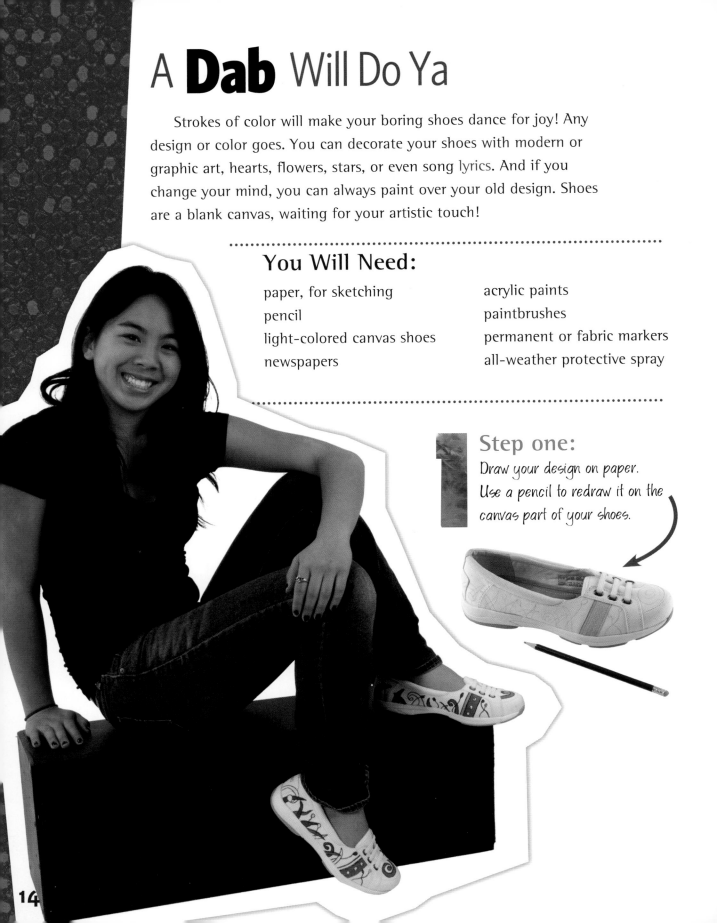

14

Step two:

Remove shoelaces, if possible. Fill shoes with bunched-up newspapers.

Step three:

Place a flat piece of newspaper under each shoe. Use paints and brushes to make your design, rotating the paper as you go. Repeat with other shoe. Let shoes dry.

Step four:

Use markers to highlight your creation. Add details, outlines, or write a message on your shoes. Allow to dry.

❋ *Variations*:

- Cover dark-colored shoes with two coats of white paint before decorating them. Let dry between coats.
- Add rhinestones by squirting a dot of puffy paint on your shoe. Then press a rhinestone into the paint.

Step five:

In a well-ventilated area, spray shoes with all-weather protective spray.

lyrics—the words of a song

Toe **Tapper**

These music-covered shoes will make your feet want to sing. Wear these shoes to toe-tapping events or whenever you just want to carry a tune. You'll feel and look like a rock star in these sweet-singing shoes!

You Will Need:

- patent leather or vinyl shoes
- fine sandpaper
- damp paper towel
- newspapers
- sheet music
- pan or bowl of water
- outdoor decoupage glue
- foam brush
- rhinestone buckle
- craft glue
- all-weather protective spray

Step one:

Rub each shoe gently with sandpaper. Remove any dust with damp paper towel.

Step two:
Fill shoes with crumpled newspapers. Place a piece of newspaper under each shoe.

Step three:
Tear or cut sheet music into strips. Soften paper by soaking each piece in water for five to 20 seconds. Shake off excess water.

Tip: If you don't have original sheet music, you can use laser-printed copies from approved Web sites. Test your copy with decoupage to check for smears. Laser copies will not need to be soaked. Avoid printing from an inkjet printer. The ink will smear.

continue on next page

Step four:

With foam brush, cover a small area of one shoe with decoupage. Carefully place damp sheet music over glued area. Brush with more decoupage.

Tip: Decoupage glue can be messy. Remove any drips or messes with a damp paper towel.

Step five:

Continue covering both shoes, overlapping music pieces. Let dry completely.

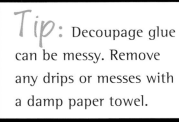

Step six:

Spray shoes with protective spray. Glue on buckle.

✸ *Variations*:

- If you're not a musical person, cover your shoes with other papers. Use stamps, wrapping paper, magazine pictures, or comic books.
- Canvas shoes can be used too, but you don't need to sand them. Remember that covering canvas shoes with decoupage can make them stiffer and tighter. You may want to start with shoes that are a half-size larger than you normally wear.

Purr-fect Shoes

Your feet will roar with delight in these stylish animal print shoes. These shoes show off your wild side! Impress your friends when you show up in these feminine feline shoes.

You Will Need:

tissue paper
any kind of shoe
pencil
scissors
animal print fabric

two-sided tape
fabric glue
small foam paintbrush
decorative ribbon
metal accents

1 Step one:

Place a piece of tissue paper under part of a shoe, such as the toe. Use the pencil to trace the shoe's outline on the tissue paper. Make the outline about ½ inch wider than the shoe. Draw the outline slightly larger to make sure you don't come up short later.

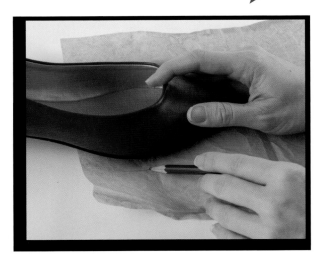

Step two:

Cut out pattern. Using the shoe as a template, trim the pattern to match exactly. Repeat until the whole shoe is done. Mark the patterns to keep pieces straight.

Step three:

Use the two-sided tape to attach pattern pieces onto the front of the fabric. Cut the pattern shapes out of the fabric.

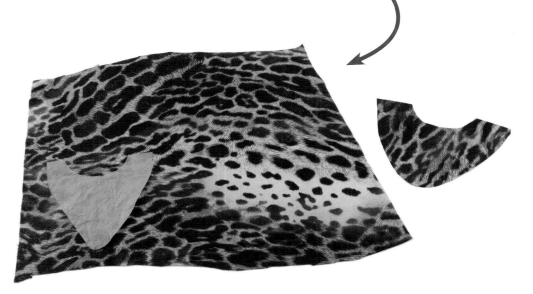

continue on next page

Step four:

Use the paintbrush to spread a thin coat of glue over a small part of the shoe. Cover the shoe with matching fabric piece. Continue to cover both shoes. Let dry.

Step five:

Carefully apply glue where the fabric pieces meet. Press ribbon onto glue and hold until it is set. Continue gluing until all edges are secured.

Step six:

Glue metal accents to the toes of the shoes.

Tip: Cut slits in the fabric if it bunches up while gluing. Overlap flaps to lay flat.

 Variations:

- You don't have to limit yourself to animal prints. Most fabric will do. But avoid using thick fabrics such as corduroy or thin fabrics like silk.
- Cover only one part of the shoe (such as the toe).

Flowers for Your Feet

Dress up any shoes by adding these classy rose shoe clips. They look great on ballet flats, flip-flops, or slippers. Your feet will be as beautiful as a bouquet!

You Will Need:

2 18- to 24-inch pieces of wire
   ribbon, ½ to 1 inch wide
felt
hot glue and glue gun
clip-on earring backs

Step one:

Fold one ribbon end over ½ inch. This will be the rose's base.

continue on next page

Step two:
Pinch the folded end of the ribbon to hold the wires tight.

Step three:
Starting at the unfolded end, push the bottom of the ribbon up the wire toward the fold.

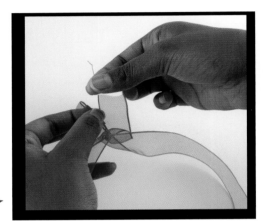

Step four:
Continue pushing the ribbon along the wire. Let the ribbon spiral naturally.

Step five:
Wrap the wire around the folded edge of the ribbon to make a short stem. Repeat with other ribbon.

Step six:

Cut two felt circles half the size of the rose. Hot glue an earring back onto each felt circle.

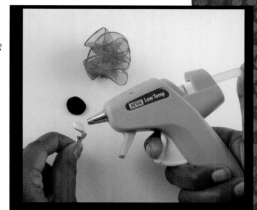

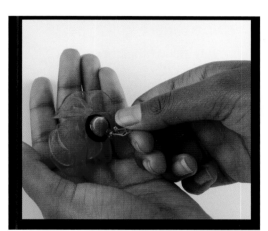

Step seven:

Cover the non-clip side of the felt circle with glue. Press to bottom of flower and hold until set. Clip onto shoes.

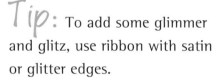

Tip: To add some glimmer and glitz, use ribbon with satin or glitter edges.

Princess Slippers

Don't let cold toes keep you down! These feather-covered slippers will make you feel like a sleeping beauty. You'll be on your feet and ready to sing while fitted with your fuzzy fashions.

You Will Need:

scissors
1 24-inch feather boa
hot glue and glue gun
bedroom slippers

2 silk flowers
wire cutters
2 1-inch rhinestones

Step one:
Cut boa in half. Glue the cut ends of the boa to prevent feathers from falling off.

Step two:

Apply a line of hot glue where the top of the slipper and the sole meet. Carefully press one end of the boa into the glue.

Tip: Keep fingers on the boa's **core**, to keep from burning fingers.

Step three:

Curve the boa and continue gluing and pressing the next row. Make a zigzag pattern working toward the toe. Repeat with other slipper.

Step four:

Cut off the flower stem with a wire cutter. Apply a dot of glue to the center of the flower. Press a rhinestone into the glue and hold until set. Repeat with other flower.

Step five:

Apply a small amount of hot glue to the slipper. Press flower into glue and hold until set. Repeat with other slipper.

core—the inner part of the boa to which feathers are attached

Twinkle Toes

Get a set of slip-ons that match your sparkling personality! You'll stand out in a crowd while wearing these glittering shoes. Any color glitter will do. Show off the real you while staying stylish.

You Will Need:

patent leather or vinyl shoes
newspaper
foam brush
glossy decoupage glue
loose glitter
all-weather protective spray

Step one:
Remove insoles from shoes.

Step two:
Place shoes on the newspaper. Stuff the insides of the shoes with crumpled newspaper.

 ### Step three:
Use foam brush to paint decoupage directly onto shoe.

 ### Step four:
Sprinkle loose glitter over the wet shoes. Tap off any excess glitter.

 ### Step five:
Paint a thin layer of decoupage glue over shoes. Let dry.

❈ *Variation*:
• You don't need to cover your whole shoe in glitter. Tape off an area of your shoe to cover in glitter, such as the toe or a star shape.

 ### Step six:
Spray shoes with protective spray. Let dry. Replace insoles.

Glossary

absorb (ab-ZORB)—to soak up

core (KOR)—the inner part of the boa to which feathers are attached

decoupage (day-koo-PAHZH)—a liquid glue used in craft projects

insole (IN-sohl)—the inner lining of a shoe or boot

lyrics (LIHR-iks)—the words of a song

sole (SOLE)—the bottom of your shoe

theme (THEEM)—a central idea for a party or event that is reflected in the decoration, food, and dress

vintage (VIN-tij)—from the past

Read **More**

Kelley, K. C. *Fashion Design Secrets.* Reading Rocks! Mankato, Minn.: Child's World, 2009.

Laughlin, Kara L. *Beautiful Bags for the Crafty Fashionista.* Fashion Craft Studio. Mankato, Minn.: Capstone Press, 2012.

Maurer, Tracy. *Fabulous Fashion Crafts.* Creative Crafts for Kids. Vero Beach, Fla.: Rourke Pub., 2009.

Internet Sites

FactHound offers a safe, fun way to find Internet sites related to this book. All of the sites on FactHound have been researched by our staff.

Here's all you do:

Visit *www.facthound.com*

Type in this code: 9781429665544

 Super-cool stuff! Check out projects, games and lots more at www.capstonekids.com

Index